Medieval Times

SUZANNE MUIR

Editorial Board

David Booth • Joan Green • Jack Booth

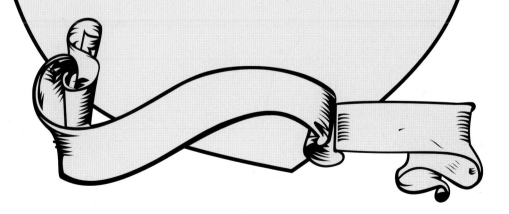

This book is dedicated to:
Zayd and Haytham

HOUGHTON MIFFLIN HARCOURT

www.SteckVaughn.com
800-289-4490

10801 N. Mopac Expressway
Building # 3
Austin, TX 78759
1.800.531.5015

Steck-Vaughn is a trademark of HMH Supplemental Publishers Inc.
registered in the United States of America and/or other jurisdictions.
All inquiries should be mailed to HMH Supplemental Publishers Inc.,
P.O. Box 27010, Austin, TX 78755.

Ru'bicon
www.rubiconpublishing.com

Project Editor: Miriam Bardswich, Maggie Goh
Editorial Assistant: Amy Land
Art/Creative Director: Jennifer Drew
Assistant Art Director: Jen Harvey
Designer: Gabriela Castillo

Cover image–CORBIS

11 12 13 14 15   6 5 4 3 2

Medieval Times
ISBN 13: 978-1-4190-2385-9
ISBN 10: 1-4190-2385-3

Printed in Singapore

CONTENTS

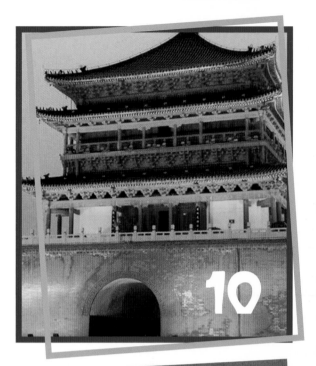

10

16

30

Knights and castles, kings and queens
water wheels and torture machines.
The Golden Age and Dark Age too
from London Tower to Baghdad zoo.

Travel along with a caravan
to far-off cities like Chang'an.
Catch a camel, ride a horse.
Look around for bandits, of course.

Avoid the plague and take good care
Live in a palace or visit the fair.
Polish your armor until it shines.
You'll find it all during medieval times.

Historians call the period from 500 to 1500 A.D. the Middle Ages or medieval times.

STRANGE but True MEDIEVAL FACTS

warm up

Imagine you are from the future. What customs do we have that might seem strange to people in the future?

Europeans thought that the world was flat, and that if you sailed too far you might fall off the edge.

Doctors in Europe believed that illness was caused by too much blood. They put leeches on patients to suck out the extra blood. Yuck! Some people bled to death.

In England during the 1300s, the length of the toe of your shoe would tell people how important you were. The king's shoes had the longest toes.

The length of clothing determined how rich people were. If you could afford to buy a lot of material, you wore long shirts and robes. If you were poor, you wore a shorter shirt and pants.

Dolls were made with a hollow center, and a bird or mouse was sewn inside to make it come to life and move.

The city of Baghdad was burned to the ground by Mongols in 1258. Almost everyone in the city was killed and many of the books in the libraries were lost.

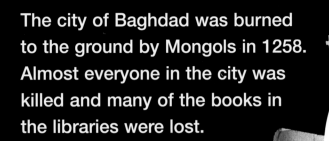

In China, during the Tang Dynasty, when Emperor Gaozong (628-683 A.D.) died, 61 kings came to his funeral!

In medieval Europe, the night before All Saints' Day was known as All Hallows Eve (Halloween). On that night, poor people demanded food from the rich — and threatened to burn down their barns if they did not receive food. How's that for "trick or treat"?

wrap up

1. Choose two of these facts. Write a headline for a newspaper report about the event.

2. Imagine that you are living 100 years in the future. Write two "Strange but True" stories about something that is done today — for example, why we cut people open for surgery.

For Sale

Medieval Royal Homes

warm up

Palaces were homes for kings and queens. With a partner, brainstorm words to describe palaces.

Bigger is better, especially when it comes to dream homes! Here are some of the finest medieval homes on the market. Kings, queens, princes, and princesses only, please.

Abbasid Palace

Baghdad, Iraq

Relax by the many fountains and rose gardens of this fabulous palace. If only the best will do, this place is for you! Move fast. This one won't last long!

- Many different rooms, all with heavy silk curtains for privacy
- All rooms decorated with expensive furniture and silk cushions
- Beautiful brickwork and archways
- Protected by 100 lions and four elephants
- Close to the action of this exciting city
- Near the mosque and the bazaar
- Full staff of 2,000 to serve you and your family

mosque: *Muslim place of worship*

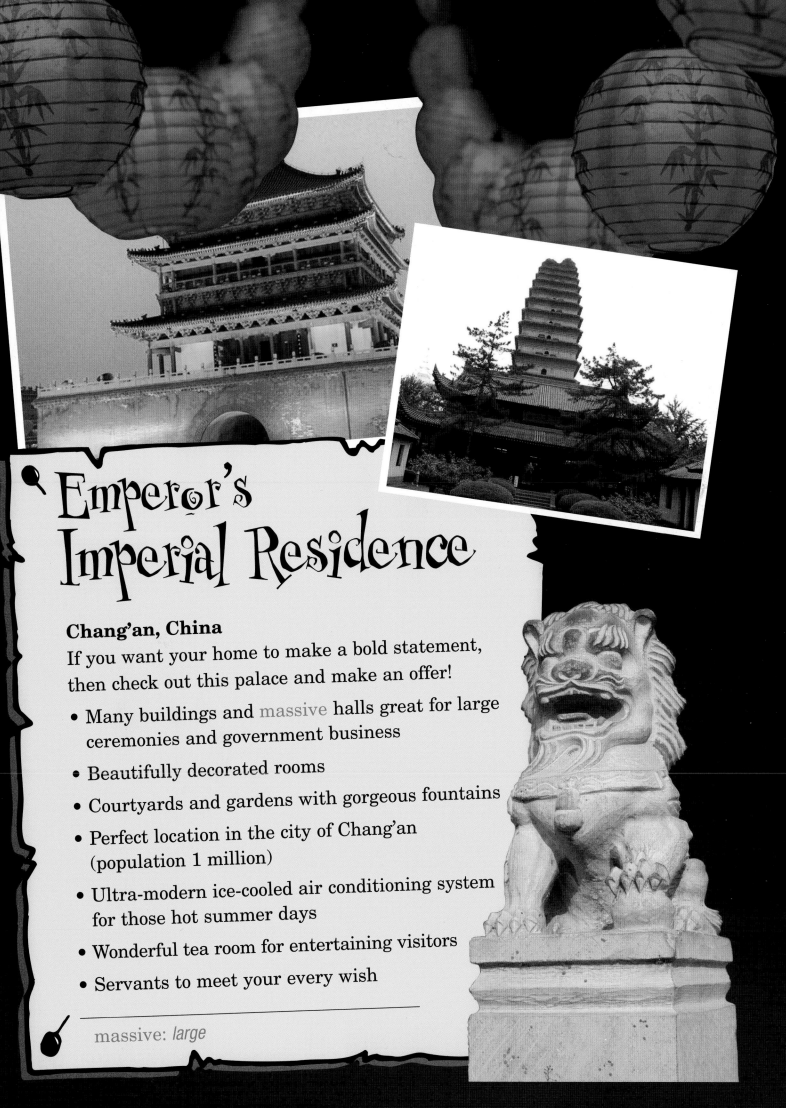

Emperor's Imperial Residence

Chang'an, China

If you want your home to make a bold statement, then check out this palace and make an offer!

- Many buildings and massive halls great for large ceremonies and government business

- Beautifully decorated rooms

- Courtyards and gardens with gorgeous fountains

- Perfect location in the city of Chang'an (population 1 million)

- Ultra-modern ice-cooled air conditioning system for those hot summer days

- Wonderful tea room for entertaining visitors

- Servants to meet your every wish

---

massive: *large*

Tower of London

London, England

Great for anyone who has ever wanted to live like a king or queen! This multi-use building is very roomy and loaded with special features, including:

- State-of-the-art security with a drawbridge, turrets, and moat

- Right on the River Thames. Drive your boat to the front doors!

- Wonderful for entertaining visiting kings

- Several secret rooms and passageways

- Fireplaces in almost every room for those frosty winter nights

- Fully-equipped torture chamber and prison cells

- Comes with a full staff, horses, and a boat

FYI

The toilets in medieval castles were called "garderobes." They were little rooms that had a stone seat with a hole in it.

After people used this "toilet," the waste would flow out into the moat. Imagine the smell!

wrap up

1. Which palace would you buy? Write a sentence or two explaining why.

2. Sketch a picture of your dream castle.

WEB CONNECTIONS

Now that you know how royalty lived during the Middle Ages, use the Internet to research how serfs (servants) lived. Type **"medieval serfs"** into a search engine and write a paragraph about what you learned.

Saladin and Richard The Lionheart

Illustrated by
JEREMY BENNISON

THE CRUSADES WERE A SERIES OF WARS FOUGHT IN THE MIDDLE AGES. EUROPEAN ARMIES INVADED THE HOLY LAND TO RECLAIM JERUSALEM FROM THE MUSLIM EMPIRE. IN THIS BATTLE DURING THE THIRD CRUSADE, SALADIN'S ARMY FACED THE SMALLER ARMY LED BY KING RICHARD I.

Why was King Richard known as the Lionheart? Discuss.

MY LOYAL ARMY. WE HAVE OUTNUMBERED THE CRUSADERS. VICTORY WILL SOON BE OURS.

FORWARD!

ONWARD MEN. WE ARE FIGHTING TO RECAPTURE THE HOLY LAND FOR EUROPE!

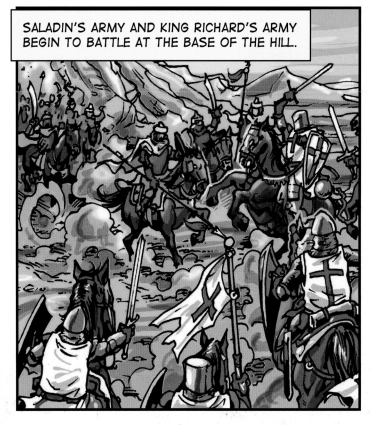

SALADIN'S ARMY AND KING RICHARD'S ARMY BEGIN TO BATTLE AT THE BASE OF THE HILL.

KING RICHARD WATCH OUT! YOUR HORSE!

MY NOBLE STEED. YOU HAVE SERVED ME WELL. I CAN FIGHT SALADIN'S ARMY ON FOOT.

KING RICHARD! TAKE MY HORSE OR YOU TOO WILL SURELY FALL IN THIS BATTLE.

NO, GOOD KNIGHT, I WILL BE ALL RIGHT. YOU MUST GO FORWARD.

MEANWHILE, ONE OF SALADIN'S MEN HAS TOLD HIM THAT KING RICHARD'S HORSE HAS DIED IN BATTLE.

FALL BACK, MEN. KING RICHARD'S STEED HAS FALLEN. THIS IS A MOST UNFAIR TURN OF EVENTS.

SALADIN, WE MUST TAKE ADVANTAGE OF HIS BAD LUCK. THIS IS OUR CHANCE TO CAPTURE THE KING OR KILL HIM ...

ONE YEAR LATER, A TRUCE IS FORMED WITH SALADIN ALLOWING THE CHRISTIANS PASSAGE TO AN IMPORTANT RELIGIOUS SITE IN JERUSALEM.

wrap up

1. With a group of friends act out the battle in the story. Show the two kings' kindness toward each other.

2. Imagine you are King Richard and write a letter to Saladin thanking him for his gift of horses.

WEB CONNECTIONS

Use the Internet to research the Crusades. Create a timeline of the main battles.

Women of Power!

Check out these brave medieval women

warm up

Scan the headings beside each of these women. Think of a modern woman who could fit that description.

As they say, "a woman's work is never done." This was especially true in the Middle Ages. It was a hard time to be a woman. Still, these seven fearless females managed to take charge!

The Rebel

At the age of 12, JOAN OF ARC (1412-1431) began hearing voices telling her to help the French fight the English. She dressed as a boy and joined the army. She led the French to victory over the English in 1429. A few years later, people accused her of being a witch and she was burned at the stake.

Illustrations by Colin Mayne

The Businesswoman

KHADIJA (555-619 A.D.) owned her own trading company in Arabia. She traded goods from Arabia to India. She also asked for her husband's hand in marriage. Her husband, Muhammed, was 20 years younger than her.

CHECKPOINT

A.D. stands for "anno domini" (meaning "in the year of our Lord"). Some people also used CE which stands for "Common Era".

The Queen

ELEANOR OF AQUITAINE (1122-1204) was the wife of King Louis VII of France and one of the greatest female rulers. She was very well-educated, which was unusual for a woman at this time. She shocked everyone when she organized over 300 women to help fight in the Crusades.

The Empress

WU ZETIAN (625-705 A.D.) was a Tang dynasty empress in China. She was known for building Buddhist temples. It was unusual for a woman to be empress in those days. She was always scared that someone was trying to take over her rule.

The Poet

RABIA AL-ADAWIYYA (717-801 A.D.) was born as a slave girl in Iraq and was freed by her owner. Although many men proposed marriage to her she refused them all. She became a well-known writer of poetry. Her favorite subjects were love, nature, and beauty.

The Brave One

FA MULAN (581-618 A.D.) was a girl in medieval China. She went into battle because her father was sick and she had no brothers. She was said to be a great soldier who was as brave and strong as any man.

While Fa Mulan was fighting battles, many other girls were either working on their parents' farm or if they came from wealthy families they were learning an art like sewing, painting, or cooking.

Although it seems very young to us, medieval Chinese girls would usually get married at the age of about 13!

CHECK-POINT

What do you think honor means?

Fa Mulan

A girl dressed as a boy
To save her father's honor

She fought in battles strong
As tough as any brother

The emperor rewarded her
With a high position

But she longed for home
That was her decision

In books and children's hearts
Her story carries on

The brave and clever girl
The daring Fa Mulan

The African Queen

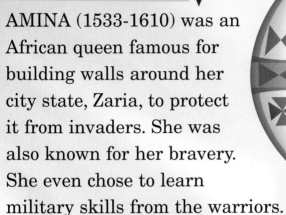

AMINA (1533-1610) was an African queen famous for building walls around her city state, Zaria, to protect it from invaders. She was also known for her bravery. She even chose to learn military skills from the warriors.

Ladies First?

- In the Muslim world, Islam gave women many rights. These are just a few of them: to own her own property, to run her own business, to get divorced, and to keep her own money. Women worked as scribes, doctors, teachers, and even judges.

- In Europe, women had few rights and these depended on their wealth. Peasant women worked in the fields with men, but did not go to school. Noblewomen did not work, but they did go to school.

- China's Tang dynasty was a period of greater freedom for women. Girls did not bind their feet as they had in other times. They were allowed to study the arts like music, painting, and singing.

wrap up

1. Choose your favorite medieval woman and write a poem based on her life.

2. Make a list of the qualities that each of the women had.

Mother Goose's

Learn the real story behind these nursery rhymes

warm up

Have you ever started a rumor or had a rumor spread about you? Share your experiences with a partner.

Most of our favorite nursery rhymes came from medieval Europe. They were a way for the peasants and common people to spread rumors about royalty without getting into trouble. Here are a few examples ...

Humpty Dumpty

Humpy Dumpty sat on a wall;
Humpty Dumpty had a great fall.
All the king's horses and all the king's men
Couldn't put Humpty together again!

· · · · · · · · · · · · · · · ·

This rhyme is said to be about King Richard III of England who had a humped back. He was riding his horse named "Wall" in his last battle when he fell off and was hacked up by the enemy. Even though they tried, none of his men could save him.

Secrets

Jack Be Nimble

Jack be nimble;
Jack be quick;
Jack jump over the candlestick.

• • • • • • • • • • • • •

In medieval times, jumping over a lit candlestick was a celebration game at weddings. If the flame went out when you jumped over it, you were in for a year of bad luck. If the candle stayed lit it meant good luck for the next year. If your pants caught on fire, that meant you were really unlucky at that moment!

Three Blind Mice

Three blind mice,
Three blind mice
See how they run,
See how they run!
They all ran after the farmer's wife
She cut off their tails with a carving knife.
Did you ever see such a thing in your life,
As three blind mice?

• • • • • • • • • • • • • •

This nursery rhyme is said to be about Queen Mary I of England. She disliked three noblemen and had them burned at the stake. People sang this song to speak out about her harsh ways.

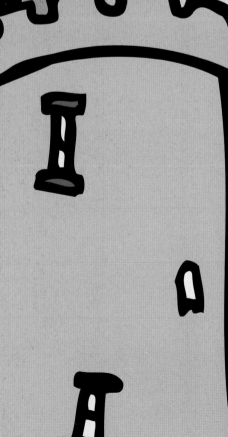

Old King Cole

Old King Cole was a merry old soul,
And a merry old soul was he.
He called for his pipe,
And he called for his bowl,
And he called for fiddlers three.

· · · · · · · · · · · · · · · ·

This rhyme is about an English king who was popular and well-liked by the people. He enjoyed music and his daughter was said to be a beautiful singer.

Ring Around the Rosie

Ring around the Rosie,
A pocket full of posies,
Ashes! Ashes!
We all fall down!

· · · · · · · · · · · · · · · ·

"Ring Around the Rosie" was really about the plague. A pocket full of posies refers to flowers and herbs that people held to their noses to avoid catching the plague which they thought was spread though "bad air." Also, plague victims would cough up blood which looked like "ashes." Many people fell down dead because of the plague.

plague: *very bad disease that spreads easily*

wrap up

1. Choose one of these nursery rhymes and do a dramatic reading for a kindergarten class.

2. Think of a news story you have heard recently. Write your own four-line rhyme about it.

Discover This!

Medieval Explorers
Uncover a Whole New World

warm up

Think about how long it must have taken to travel in medieval times compared to today.

- Aud the Viking Queen
- Marco Polo
- Ibn Battuta
- Cheng Ho

Europe

Asia

Africa

Australia

They didn't have jumbo jets, space shuttles, or even cars, but these four medieval explorers were still able to cover a lot of ground. Take a look at where their adventurous spirits took them!

Aud the "Deep-Minded" Viking Queen (834-900)

Where: From Norway to Scotland, Ireland, and Iceland

How: By ship

Why: After her son and her husband died, Queen Aud organized this trip to find a new place to live. She was one of Iceland's most important settlers.

Pssst: Aud was called "Deep-Minded" because she was so smart.

Marco Polo (1254-1324)

Where: From Italy to China

How: He traveled by ship and by caravan

Why: Marco Polo was one of the first Westerners to travel the Silk Route. In China he discovered new foods like pasta and ice cream. He was known as "the man with a million stories" and he wrote a book about his explorations.

Pssst: Christopher Columbus owned a copy of Marco Polo's book!

Ibn Battuta (1304-1369)

Where: From Morocco to Asia, Africa, and Europe

How: By camel, caravan, and ship

Why: Ibn Battuta made the Hajj trip to Mecca to learn about different peoples. He traveled for 29 years. He wrote a book about all the interesting cultures that he found.

Pssst: On his travels, Ibn Battuta was almost beheaded by a tyrant ruler!

Hajj: a trip made for religious reasons to Mecca

Cheng Ho (Zheng He) (1371-1433)

Where: From China to India, Ceylon, Vietnam, Africa, and Australia

How: He was the leader of a fleet of over 50 ships

Why: Cheng Ho was ordered to make trade visits to several countries. He brought back spices, jewels, and exotic animals. He made seven voyages.

Pssst: Cheng Ho used lanterns and gongs to communicate between all his ships.

wrap up

Draw a picture of one method of transportation used at this time: ship, camel, or horse.

WEB CONNECTIONS

Using the Internet, find out more about one of these explorers. Using this information, write a short biography about the explorer.

The Sky is Falling

A Tale From Medieval China

warm up

Check out the title of this story. What do you think this story will be about?

A long time ago in China, some children were out playing in the fields. Suddenly, something fell on their heads. The children stopped playing and looked up at the sky. They gasped in fear, and ran into the village to tell the Wise Woman what they had seen.

"Wise Woman! Wise Woman!" they shouted. "The sky is falling! Come and see!"

Wise Woman smiled calmly at the children. "Don't worry, children," she said. "Go and collect all the pieces of the sky that have fallen and I will sew them back together."

The children ran back to the fields and began to gather up the pieces of sky from the ground. They carried them back to Wise Woman.

"Wise Woman, the spring festival is only a few days away," said the children. "The sky must be fixed by then, or our village will be in disgrace."

Wise Woman nodded and said, "Do not worry, children. I will take care of it."

CHECKPOINT

How do you think Wise Woman is going to fix the sky?

The next day the children ran outside to play. It was a beautiful spring day. The children looked up at the sky. It was clear and blue. The children clapped in delight. "Wise Woman has fixed the sky," they sang out. "Thank you, Wise Woman!" And they skipped happily off to play.

That night, after the sun had gone down, the children went outside to check the sky again. Their mouths dropped open in amazement.

Usually the sky was a deep, dark black. On this night it was covered with tiny dots of light. Wise Woman had patched together the missing pieces of sky with bright twinkling lights!

"How beautiful," the children exclaimed. "Wise Woman is so smart. We will have the best spring festival in the land!"

From then on, each clear night as the sun fades, the stars begin to twinkle in the darkness, thanks to a Wise Woman who lived long ago in a village in China.

wrap up

1. In the voice of one of the children, write a journal entry about the day the sky fell.

2. Write your own myth that explains another event, for example, why there are rainbows, or thunderstorms, etc.

Hit the Road!
Queen Zubaydah's Royal Route

warm up

With a partner, brainstorm all the ways that people travel today.

Queen Zubaydah was a kind and generous queen who lived in the 700s. She was married to the Caliph Harun Al-Rashid. Read about her most important project in this letter she wrote to a senior government official.

Caliph: *ruler in the Muslim world*

Dear Vizier,

I have been thinking about our talk the other day. I agree there is a problem for those who want to travel from Baghdad to Mecca for the Hajj trip. The desert is too hot and dry for such a long trip.

I think I have an answer. We will build a road and beside that road we will dig a water canal. Along the way we will make a caravansary for the people to stop and take a break, collect water, eat a meal, and sleep. My husband, the Caliph, agrees with me.

Please hire the workers to start building the road and canal right away.

Peace be upon you,

Queen Zubaydah

Mecca: *holiest Muslim city in present-day Saudi Arabia*
Hajj: *a trip made for religious reasons to Mecca*

CHECK-POINT

Can you tell from the sentence what a "caravansary" is? Check the FYI to see if you were right.

:FYI

A hotel in the Islamic medieval world was called a "caravansary." They were large buildings where travelers on their way to Mecca could spend the night. There was an open area in the center where people could "park" their camels and horses.

Some caravansaries even had a post office to mail letters!

wrap up

1. Find Baghdad and Mecca on a map. What countries are they in? What countries are next door?

2. Write a short newspaper report telling people about the queen's idea for a road. Include a headline.

Scheherazade's 1001 Nights

warm up

With a partner, discuss your favorite fairy tales from your childhood.

A long time ago in an Arabian land, there lived a mighty but dangerous king. The king had a wicked streak that caused great distress in the kingdom. He had married many times. Each time he married, he grew angry with his wife, and had her put to death.

Everyone in the kingdom was very sad. They had lost too many of their sisters and daughters to this crazy king.

One day, Scheherazade, a brave and beautiful woman, decided to put an end to the king's madness. She had a brilliant idea and thought she would be able to solve the problem.

Scheherazade went to her father, a vizier, and told him: "My noble father

The vizier was shocked and alarmed. "Oh by Allah's grace! These are the words that I do not want to hear. My beloved daughter, don't you know what the king does with all his wives? This is a death wish!" the vizier cried.

"Do not be afraid, father. I have a plan," Scheherazade said. "Trust me."

CHECKPOINT

What do you think her plan is?

The vizier loved his daughter very much. He was very sad, but he agreed to let her try to save the women in the kingdom. He took Scheherazade's proposal to the king, who agreed to

Scheherazade was the most beautiful bride that the king had ever seen. After a very grand wedding, the newlyweds retired to the royal bedroom. As they were getting ready for bed, they heard a small knock on the door. It was Scheherazade's little sister, Dunyazad.

"My King, forgive me for bothering you. Every night my sister tells me a story to help me sleep. I fear that if I don't hear her beautiful stories I shall never sleep again," little Dunyazad said. "Could Scheherazade just tell me one story, please?"

"Very well," the king said with a sigh.

Scheherazade sat down and began to

That night she told the tale of Aladdin and the magic lamp. She wove an exciting story about magical genies and flying carpets. The king liked it so much that he was on the edge of his seat. His eyes were wide with amazement.

CHECKPOINT
How can you tell that the king is enjoying the story?

Suddenly, just before the story ended, Scheherazade stopped. "We will have to continue tomorrow night, my dear Dunyazad," she said sweetly to her sister.

"Oh no!" shouted the king. "I just *have* to know what happens next. Your story is so wonderful!"

CHECKPOINT
What do you think is going to happen next?

Scheherazade yawned. "I am sorry, Your Highness, but I am too tired. You will have to wait until tomorrow night to hear the end of the story."

The king was eager to hear the rest of the story. For the first time, he did not kill his bride. Instead, he fell into a deep sleep. He woke up the next morning looking forward to listening to another story.

That night, and every night after that, for 1001 nights, Dunyazad knocked

on the door of the royal bedroom and, together with the king, listened to Scheherazade's tales. She told of the adventures of Sinbad the sailor and the sea monsters, of Ali Baba and the 40 thieves, and many other exciting stories.

On the 1001 night, Scheherazade turned to the king and said, "I'm afraid tonight is the last night for the story, my King. The people say that you kill every wife on the first night, so why have you allowed me to live for so

CHECKPOINT
Why did the king allow her to live?

The king turned red with embarrassment. "Oh, my beautiful Scheherazade! I was such a monster!" he cried. "At first, I kept you because I only wanted to hear more stories. But with each passing night, I fell more and more in love with you. I could never live without you. I'm so sorry for the evil things I have done."

Scheherazade was overjoyed. She ran to tell her father the wonderful news. The king's evil ways had been broken. The kingdom rang with joy at the news.

"My daughter, I didn't know how you were going to do it," said the vizier with amazement.

"A good story lives on despite all else," Scheherazade said to her father with a smile.

wrap up

1. What do you learn about the king at the beginning of the story? How does he change by the end? Answer in two sentences.

2. With a partner, create a storyboard with three or four frames that continue the story.

BAD BEHAVIOR

Crime & Punishment in Medieval Times

warm up

Think of the last time you were punished. What was your "crime"? Was the punishment fair? Explain to a partner.

Medieval Laws

Some of these laws may sound silly, but you sure wouldn't want to be caught breaking them! Medieval punishment was almost always severe.

Nowhere to Hide

"I, King Edward I, do decree that all the trees along the main roads shall be cut down so that bandits cannot hide and attack people." Edward also introduced the idea of village police officers in England.

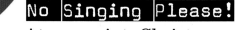

You Are What You Wear

Peasants were told that they could not wear the same clothing styles as the people of the noble class.

No Singing Please!

At one point, Christmas caroling, which included dancing, was forbidden by the Church. People stopped singing in church and began to sing from house to house.

34

Witches Everywhere

In Europe, many women and some men were accused of being witches because they did something as simple as using herbs to cure an illness. As punishment they were put into deep water with a stone tied around them. If they drowned, they were declared to be innocent. If they floated, they were to be declared a witch and were killed.

WITCHES

You Want to Fight?

Sometimes the victim of the crime and the person accused would fight. Whoever won was pronounced as innocent and the other was punished.

GUILTY GUILTY!

Trial by Ordeal

When someone was accused of a crime he or she was tried by ordeal. Officials gave the accused person burning hot metal to hold. If the burn healed they would be saved. If it did not, then the person was guilty!

FYI

Bakers who sold moldy bread or cheated their customers were dragged through the streets while people threw things at them.

OW, THAT HURTS!

Medieval Punishment

Sometimes the good ol' days weren't so good — especially when they involved torture. People were tortured as punishment for crimes or to get information from them. The torture was usually performed in public places as a form of entertainment (and you thought reality TV was scary!).

The Stocks

A person's head and arms would be locked in the stocks. Then townspeople would throw things like rotten fruit at the person in the stocks.

Hanging Cages

Whirligig

This one was almost fun. It involved the criminals being spun around and around in a cage until they were very sick.

Dunking

People could also be punished by dunking. It involved the criminal getting repeatedly plunged into a large tub of water or river.

Victims were put into a cage and were left to hang there until they died from thirst or hunger. Depending on the season they could also freeze to death or die of heatstroke.

wrap up

1. Choose one of the medieval laws and create a poster that tells people not to break this law.

2. Arrange the above four punishments in order from bad to worst. Explain why you ranked them that way.

Medieval HOLIDAYS

warm up

What holidays do you and your classmates celebrate? Take a survey of the class.

Marian's Christmas

(December 6th)

My name is Marian. I am nine years old. My father is a nobleman. Tonight is Christmas Eve. We will go to church tonight and tomorrow morning. Then we will have a great banquet with wonderful foods. Mother took me to see the St. George play. I love the part where St. George slays the dragon. I hope I get a top for Christmas. Merry Christmas everyone!

banquet: *a large dinner of many foods and many guests*

Paper–istockphoto

Ping's Chinese New Year

My name is Ping. I am eight years old. My father is a scribe for the emperor of China. Today is Chinese New Year. Our house is decorated with red banners. This morning, we set off loud firecrackers to scare away Nian the monster. Mother has made sweets to offer the kitchen god. I stayed up really late last night because it means my parents will have a long life.

scribe: *a person who writes and copies books*

Amira's Ramadan

My name is Amira. I am ten years old. My mother is a teacher and my father is a doctor in Baghdad. Today is the last day of Ramadan, the month of fasting. Tomorrow we will celebrate Eid. We will go to the mosque for morning prayers and then go to the souk to buy food and presents. There will be storytellers and fire eaters in the souk to entertain people. Eid Mubarak! Happy Eid.

Eid: *celebration at the end of Ramadan*
mosque: *place of prayer for Muslims*
souk: *market*

Fasting

by Rumi

There is an unseen sweetness
in the stomach's emptiness.
We are lutes.

When the soundbox is filled,
no music can come forth.

When the brain and the belly
are burning from fasting,
every moment a new song rises
out of the fire.

Translation by Coleman Barks

lutes: *guitars*

Lute—Getty Images/PhotoDisc/0S34095

FYI

Rumi was a Muslim poet who lived in the Middle Ages.

wrap up

1. What is similar about these holidays? What is different?

2. Write an email to a friend describing a holiday that your family celebrates.

Hanging Out with Robin Hood

warm up

What images come to mind when you hear the name "Robin Hood"?

"Robin, wake up!" whispered Friar Tuck urgently in Robin Hood's ear. "The sheriff's men are on our track. I can hear their horses just around the bend!"

Robin Hood stood up and stretched. "What a fine morning," he exclaimed.

"I think they know that we robbed those noblemen on the path yesterday," Little John said with a worried gulp.

"Oh Tuck!" cried Marian. "I don't want to be sent back to the prince's castle. I can't live like a prisoner anymore. I would much rather roam the forest with Robin Hood and all of you." She looked around as she heard the pounding hooves growing louder.

CHECKPOINT
As you read, notice how Robin Hood acts, compared to his friends.

"It sounds like a great number of men are after us this time," laughed Robin Hood.

"How can you laugh at a time like this?" Friar Tuck cried. "There's no way we can outrun those horsemen. We'll have to fight them off."

Robin Hood walked calmly over to the tall oak trees and checked the branches. "Don't worry friends, we have the upper hand."

CHECKPOINT
What do you think Robin Hood is planning?

Without another word Robin Hood pulled an arrow from his pouch and tied a rope to it.

He sent the arrow flying up to the highest, strongest branch and watched the rope sail back down toward them.

"Up, up, and away!" Robin held his hand out to Marian. "Ladies first!"

Marian quickly climbed the rope to the lush branches above. Little John and Robin Hood followed. Friar Tuck was left on the ground. He was looking very scared. He could hear the voices of the men now. They would be there at any second.

Friar Tuck was a big man and he was not skilled at climbing trees (or ropes for that matter).

"Tuck! Tie the rope around your waist and as you climb we will pull you up," whispered Robin.

Sweat dripped off Friar Tuck's forehead.

"Uh, Robin? Did I tell you that I'm a little afraid of heights?" Tuck asked.

"Well my friend, this is the perfect time to get over it." And with that Robin and the others pulled Friar Tuck up.

Half way up, the knot slipped open around Friar Tuck's waist and he almost fell. Luckily Robin and Little John were able to grab the rope. They knotted it. Tuck was left swinging in the breeze!

"Okay Tuck, just stay there and be very still. Here they come," whispered Robin.

Tuck held on for dear life. Sweat now dripped off his face onto his robes. His feet dangled above the branches. He prayed that the sheriff's men would not look up.

Horses pounded into the clearing and the leader ordered everyone to stop. He looked at the smoking fire pit.

"They were just here!" he shouted.

"Look over there in the bush, there are some broken shrubs. They must have taken off in that direction." He pointed into the forest.

At that moment, the branch holding Tuck began to crackle as if it would break under his weight.

Tuck held his breath, ready to fall into the circle of men and be arrested for sure.

"Did you hear something?" the leader asked.

"No, just a bird I think. Come on, we're wasting time. Robin Hood's Merry Men are on foot so we can catch them for sure!"

Just as the soldiers thundered off down the path, the branch snapped and Friar Tuck fell to the ground with a thump!

Robin Hood, Maid Marian, and Little John climbed down after him.

"Are you okay, Tuck?" asked Robin Hood.

"Yes, just a little bumped, I guess," replied Friar Tuck.

"Well done! So what will we have for breakfast?" Robin Hood asked everyone as he stoked the fire.

"Robin, are you afraid of nothing in this world?" asked Little John.

"Well actually, there is one thing," Robin turned to everyone with a small smile. "Sitting below Friar Tuck in a tree!" Everyone laughed, including his dear friend Friar Tuck.

wrap up

1. Use a T-chart to compare the characteristics of Robin Hood and Friar Tuck.

2. Write a different ending to this story.

Do You Have a Medieval

Test yourself with this quiz!

1. When knights played a game called "jousting" they were:
   a) playing jokes on each other.
   b) trying to knock each other off a horse with a lance.
   c) racing to see who could ride faster.

2. A jester:
   a) brought drinks to the nobles.
   b) played musical instruments.
   c) told jokes about nobles.

3. At a medieval fair you might see:
   a) puppet shows, singers, and jugglers.
   b) pie-eating contests.
   c) a tooth puller taking out someone's tooth.
   d) a and c.

4. At a banquet the royal taster might:
   a) eat ice cream.
   b) taste the food for the king to make sure it wasn't poisoned.
   c) eat a bit of everyone's food until he was very full.

5. In the medieval Muslim world a special occasion food might be:
   a) sherbet ice cream.
   b) dates.
   c) oranges.

6. A medieval Middle Eastern instrument was:
   a) the bagpipes.
   b) the guitar.
   c) the piano.
   d) all of the above.

Mind?

7. Storytelling was famous in the Muslim world. Which story is from the medieval time period?
a) Aladdin and the Magic Lamp.
b) Jack and the Beanstalk.
c) The Three Little Pigs.

8. In Chinese medieval life, children played with:
a) kites, yo-yos, and tops.
b) rocks and sticks.
c) scooters.

9. The Chinese people in the medieval period enjoyed:
a) painting.
b) making puppet shows.
c) going on vacation.

10. In Muslim drawings, which images were forbidden?
a) geometric patterns.
b) animals and people.
c) flowers.

Turn to page 48 for the answers!

Answers to:
Do You Have a
Medieval Mind?

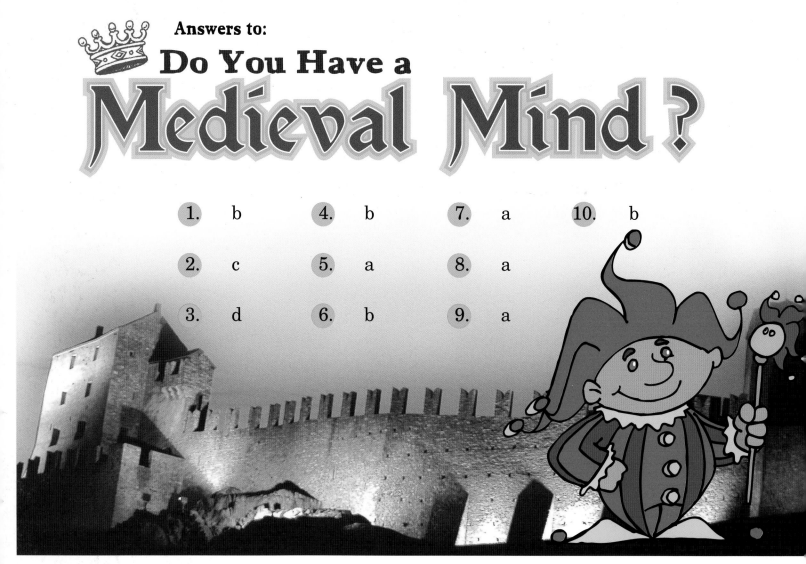

1.	b	4.	b	7.	a	10.	b
2.	c	5.	a	8.	a		
3.	d	6.	b	9.	a		

ACKNOWLEDGMENTS

The publisher gratefully acknowledges the following for permission to reprint copyrighted material in this book.

Every reasonable effort has been made to trace the owners of copyrighted material and to make due acknowledgment. Any errors or omissions drawn to our attention will be gladly rectified in future editions.

Color version of the woodcut by Flammarion copyright Roberta Weir, 1998, used with permission.

Permission to reprint Coleman Barks' translation of "Fasting" by Rumi, granted by Coleman Barks.